# THIS ACTIVITY BOOK

## BELONGS TO:

...................................................

# TIPS FOR THIS BOOK

- IN WORD SEARCH EXCERCISES HIDDEN WORDS ARE WRITTEN IN DIRECTIONS POINTED BY ARROWS:

- THIS ACTIVITY SHOULD BE DONE WITH THE HELP OF AN ADULT

- ANSWERS TO EXCERCISES CAN BE FOUND AT THE END OF THE BOOK

## Dear Customer...

I would greatly appreciate your feedback in the review section on Amazon. Every opinion means a lot to me.

**SCAN HERE TO SEE MORE**

HI! I'M THE SPHINX. I'M THE KING OF THIS COUNTRY. I REMEMBER THE VERY BEGINNING OF EGYPT. AT THE TIME WHEN I WAS MERELY A PART OF A MOUNTAIN, THE GREEN GRASS AND TREES WERE GROWING ALL AROUND ME, AND ANIMALS LIKE ANTELOPES, LIONS, ELEPHANTS, GIRAFFES AND MANY OTHER WERE STROLLING IN MY SHADE...

LATER ON, THE WEATHER BECAME HOTTER, AND EGYPT, ONCE GREEN AND BLOOMING, HAS TURNED INTO A DESERT.

IN THE ANCIENT TIMES, PEOPLE ADMIRED ME. THEY USED TO COME, BURN INCENSE, BRING GIFTS AND SING...

LATER ON, THE BARBARIANS CAME - CRUEL AND UNCIVILIZED PEOPLE, WHO WANTED TO DEMOLISH THE PYRAMIDS AND DESTROY ME. LUCKILY, THOSE DAYS ARE OVER.

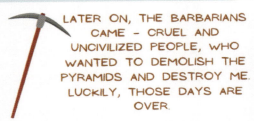

TODAY CROWDS OF PEOPLE FROM AROUND THE WORLD COME TO VISIT ME, THEY TAKE PHOTOS AND ADMIRE MY GRACE. I FEEL LIKE A KING AGAIN :)
THEY SAY I HOLD MANY MYSTERIES. TAKE A LOOK ON THE NEXT PAGES - I'VE PREPARED LOTS OF THEM JUST FOR YOU!

# LET'S GO AND SOLVE SOME RIDDLES!

# ANCIENT EGYPT

THE HISTORY OF ANCIENT EGYPT BEGAN MORE THAN 5 THOUSAND YEARS AGO. THEN, TWO KINGDOMS CONNECTED: THE UPPER AND THE LOWER EGYPT, AND THE THRONE WAS TAKEN BY THE FIRST PHARAOH - MENES

TAKE A LOOK ON THE TIMELINE BELOW. THERE ARE PRESENTED THE IMPORTANT EVENTS FROM THE PAST AND THE PRESENT.

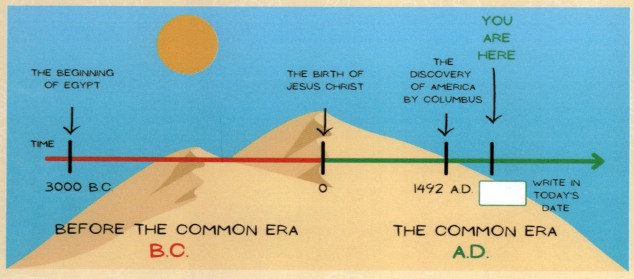

**DID YOU KNOW???**
PHARAOHS WERE THE RULERS OF ANCIENT EGYPT. THEY HAD AN ABSOLUTE POWER AND PEOPLE PERCEIVED THEM AS GODS.

**DID YOU KNOW???**
IN 30 BC ANCIENT EGYPT HAS BEEN CONQUERED AND BECAME A PART OF THE ROMAN EMPIRE.

**DID YOU KNOW???**
THE NILE, WHICH IS THE SECOND LONGEST RIVER IN THE WORLD, FLOWS IN EGYPT. IT'S 6700 KILOMETERS LONG!

SYMBOLS OF PHARAOH'S POWER

HELP THIS LITTLE EGYPTIAN GET PAST THE WILD ANIMALS OF THE NILE AND GET ON THE BOAT.

HOW IS IT POSSIBLE THAT THE GREATEST AND THE OLDEST CIVILIZATION COULD SURVIVE IN THE DESERT?

IT'S ALL THANKS TO THE NILE. FOR THOUSANDS OF YEARS, THE RIVER HAS PROVIDED A SOURCE OF IRRIGATION IN ORDER TO TRANSFORM THE DRY AREA INTO A FERTILE, AGRICULTURAL LAND. THE NILE WAS CALLED "THE RIVER OF LIFE". TAKE A LOOK BELOW TO SEE HOW EGYPTIANS BENEFITED FROM IT.

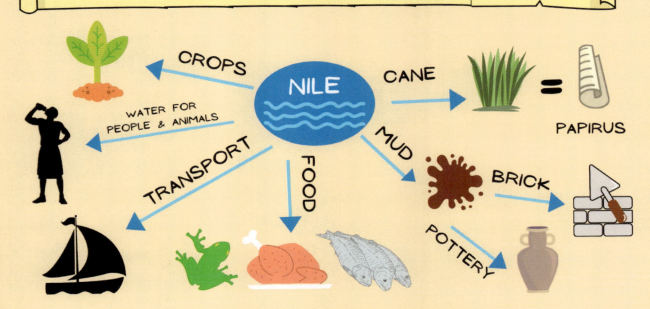

FIND 7 DIFFERENCES BETWEEN THESE PICTURES.

3 COUNT THE ITEMS AND FILL IN THE BLANKS THE CORRECT NUMBERS.

4 TRY TO FIND ALL OF THE HIDDEN ITEMS. AFTER THAT, GIVE THE TOTAL NUMBER OF THESE ITEMS.

IN ANCIENT TIMES, PEOPLE BELIEVED THAT THE SURROUNDING NATURE IS DIVINE, SO THEY WORSHIPED IT. MANY IMAGES OF EGYPTIAN GODS HAD ANIMAL-LIKE ELEMENTS OR THEY DEPICTED A MAN WITH A HEAD OF AN ANIMAL, FOR EXAMPLE ANUBIS WAS DEPICTED AS A MAN WITH A DOG'S HEAD.

**GEB**
GOD OF THE EARTH

**MUT**
QUEEN OF THE GODS AND THE MOTHER GODDESS

**OSIRIS**
GOD OF THE UNDERWORLD

**HORUS**
THE FALCON GOD OF THE SKY

**RA**
THE SUN GOD

**THOTH**
GOD OF WISDOM AND KNOWLEDGE

**BASTET**
CAT GODDESS OF LOVE AND WAR

**ANUBIS**
THE GOD OF EMBALMING AND FUNERALS

**HATHOR**
GODDESS OF LOVE AND MOTHERHOOD

THE EGYPTIAN RELIGION WAS AN EXAMPLE OF POLYTHEISM – THEY BELIEVED THAT THERE IS MORE THAN ONE GOD. THE MAIN SOURCES OF INFORMATION ABOUT THEM WERE MYTHS SPREAD ORALLY. THEY PRESENTED THE LIVES OF GODS, OFTEN RESEMBLING ORDINARY PEOPLE, WITH ALL DRAWBACKS, ILLNESSES AND SUFFERING.

IN EGYPTIAN RELIGION THERE WERE MANY GODS, GODDESSES AND DEITIES. THEY WERE THE GUARDIANS OF THE PARTICULAR SPHERES OF LIFE AND THE ELEMENTS, FOR INSTANCE WIND, AIR, WAR, HEALTH, DEATH, LOVE, ETC. PEOPLE PRAYED TO THEM AND MADE SACRIFICES IN FRONT OF THEIR STATUES IN ORDER TO RECEIVE HELP. ACCORDING TO EGYPTIANS, THE CREATOR OF THE WORLD WAS RA – THE GOD OF SUN. THAT WAS THE REASON WHY HE WAS THE MOST IMPORTANT AMONG THE GODS.

5. PAINT THE FLAG OF EGYPT.

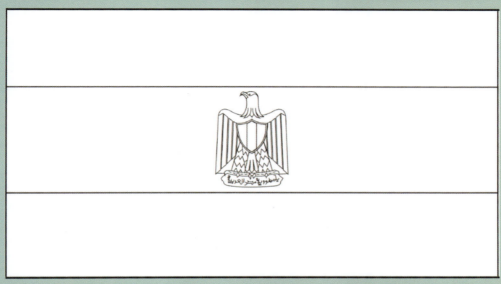

6. EGYPT IS A BIG COUNTRY IN AFRICA. TRY TO FIND IT. USE A COMPAS AND THE INFORMATIONS ON THE LEFT.

- IT IS SITUATED IN THE NORTH-EAST
- IT HAS ACCCESS TO TWO SEAS
- SUDAN IS ITS NEIGHBORING COUNTRY TO THE SOUTH

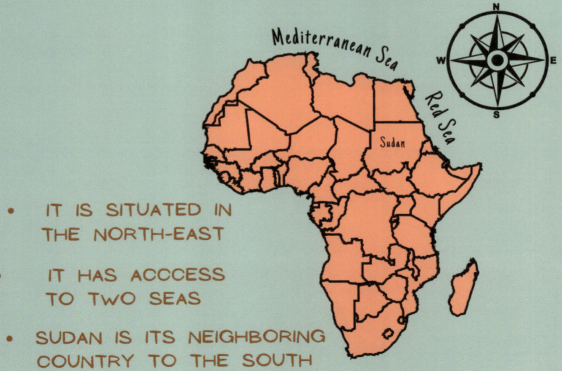

## 7. DRAW THE CROCODILE STEP BY STEP. THEN TRY TO DRAW IT IN ONE STEP.

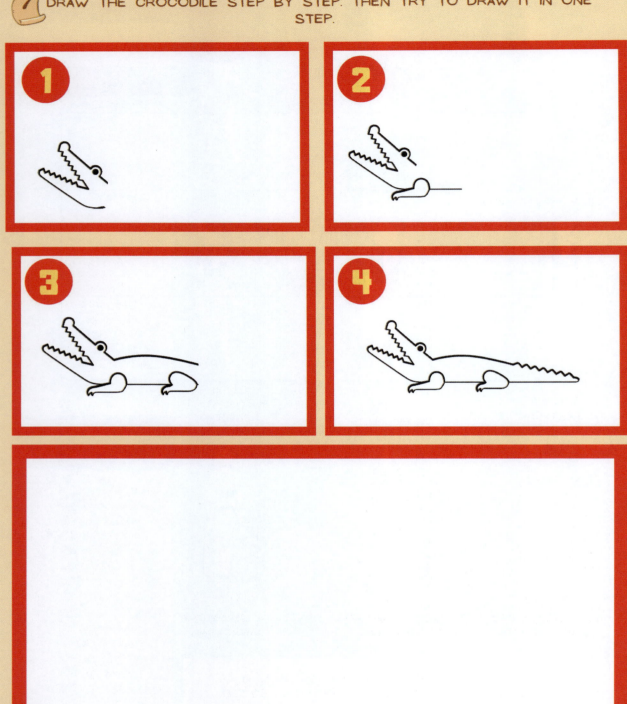

CROCODILES WERE ANIMALS WORSHIPED IN ANCIENT EGYPT. THEY WERE TO BE FOUND IN SWAMPS NEAR THE NILE. SINCE 1971, WHEN THE ASWAN DAM WAS BUILT, THEY HAVE FOUND THEIR HOME AT THE LAKE NASSER AND THEY WERE SEPARATED FROM THE RIVER. THEREFORE, THE AREA TO THE NORTH FROM ASWAN IS FREE FROM THIS DANGEROUS REPTILE.

8 TRACE THE DECORATION PATTERN ON THE VASE.

LOOK AT THE WORDLIST AND CIRCLE THE WORDS IN THE WORD SEARCH.

AMON   MUSEUM
DESERT   TALISMAN
OASIS   SETH
PHARAOH   MENES
GOLD

```
G I N P T O A S A D
O S S H A G D H S A
L E E A L T M S A U
D P L R I M U A H S
E H O A S I S M E A
S O M O M E E O A U
E H E H A D U N H S
R S N A N H M T S E
T H E E P M T E M A
O I S H E S E T H P
```

 WRITE THE WORDS IN THE CROSSWORD. LETTERS IN THE MARKED SQUARES PROVIDE THE ANSWER.

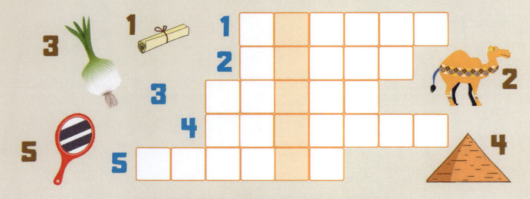

THE SOLUTION IS A PLACE IN EGYPT.

THE PROFESSION OF THE SCRIBE WAS VERY IMPORTANT IN ANCIENT EGYPT. IT WAS A VERY EDUCATED PERSON WHO KNEW THE HIEROGLYPHS WELL AND WAS ABLE TO USE THEM.
A SCRIBE WROTE CHRONICLES FOR THE RULERS, BILLS FOR THE MERCHANTS AND SPELLS AND RECIPES FOR THE DOCTORS AND PRIESTS.
ONLY BOYS COULD BECOME SCRIBES AND THEIR TRAINING LASTED A FEW YEARS.

 USE THE EMPTY SLOTS TO WRITE DOWN THE LETTERS POINTED BY THE ARROWS. WHAT WORD DID YOU GET?

# DID YOU KNOW???

HIEROGLYPHS, ALSO KNOWN AS THE SACRED SIGNS, WERE THE CHARACTERS OF THE ANCIENT EGYPTIAN WRITING SYSTEM. THE EGYPTIANS USED THEM WHENEVER THEY WANTED THE WRITTEN WORDS TO LAST. THAT'S WHY THE HIEROGLYPHS WERE OFTEN CARVED IN STONE FOUND IN THE WALLS OF TEMPLES AND TOMBS. THE TOTAL NUMBER OF THE HIEROGLYPHS WAS REALLY HIGH. IT WAS MORE THAN 700! THAT WAS THE REASON WHY ONLY FEW KNEW IT AND WERE ABLE TO USE IT.

**12** USE THE EMPTY SQUARES TO WRITE THE LETTERS MATCHING THE HIEROGLYPHS.

## DID YOU KNOW???

**13** FILL IN THE BLANKS IN SUCH A WAY THAT EACH ITEM APPEARS ONLY ONCE VERTICALLY AND HORIZONTALLY.

THE PAPYRUS, A PLANT GROWING ABUNDANTLY ACROSS THE NILE, WAS USED BY THE EGYPTIANS TO CREATE A WRITING MATERIAL.
THE STEMS WERE CUT INTO THIN STRIPS AND GLUED TOGETHER USING THE NATURAL SUBSTANCE FROM THE PAPYRUS. THEY CREATED CARDS THAT FORMED A SCROLL.
IT WAS POSSIBLE TO WRITE ON IT WITH BLACK AND RED INK.

HELP THE CARAVAN FIND THE OASIS.

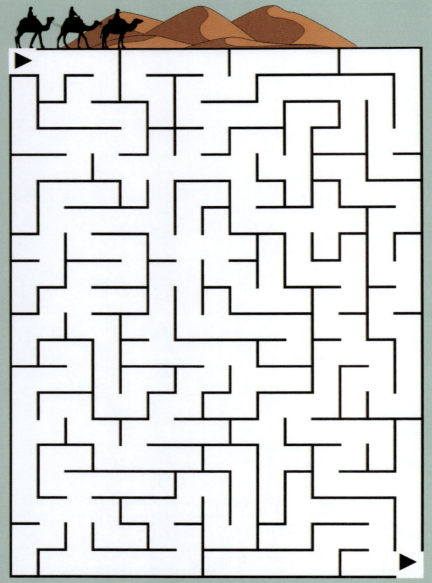

## THE SUN BOAT

THE EGYPTIANS PERCEIVED THE SKY AS A SEA, WHERE THE SUN FLOATS EVERY DAY IN A BOAT. THIS JOURNEY IS REPEATED EACH DAY FROM THE BEGINNING OF THE WORLD. RA ALSO TRAVELED IN THE SUN BOAT ALSO CALLED THE BOAT OF A MILLION YEARS. IT WAS ALSO POSSIBLE FOR THE DEAD TO TRAVEL WITH HIM TO GET TO THE OTHER WORLD.

THE EGYPTIANS DID ALL THEY COULD TO PREVENT THE DEAD BODIES FROM DECAYING. THANKS TO THE TECHNIQUES OF EMBALMING SOME MUMMIES LASTED UNTIL THE PRESENT.

THE ORGANS WERE REMOVED FROM THE BODIES, WHICH WERE LATER PUT IN SALT. AFTER A FEW WEEKS THE BODIES WERE FILLED OUT WITH SOME MATERIALS AND WRAPPED IN BANDAGES. LATER, THEY PUT THE MUMMY INTO SARCOPHAGUS.

 LOOK AT THE WORDLIST AND CIRCLE THE WORDS IN THE WORD SEARCH.

ANCIENT
CARAVAN
SAND
CURSE
THIEF
DISCOVERY
TREASURE
OSIRIS

```
T R E A S U R E E H
N S A N D S A S H R
R R A C R F A Y E A
D O S I R I S Y S C
T C C E T H I E F A
T U E N A C V T T R
T R V T R N N A I A
E S R I I A A R N V
O E O U A R R S T A
D I S C O V E R Y N
```

**BOOK OF THE DEAD**

THE BOOK OF THE DEAD WAS A PAPYRUS WITH SOME SPECIAL SPELLS. IT WAS BURIED WITH THE MUMMY TO HELP IT ON THE WAY TO THE OTHER WORLD.

**USHABTI**

USHABTI WERE SMALL FIGURES THAT WERE PLACED IN THE GRAVES WITH THE DEAD. ACCORDING TO BELIEFS, THEY WERE SUPPOSED TO DO THE WORK FOR THE DEAD ONE IN THE OTHER WORLD.

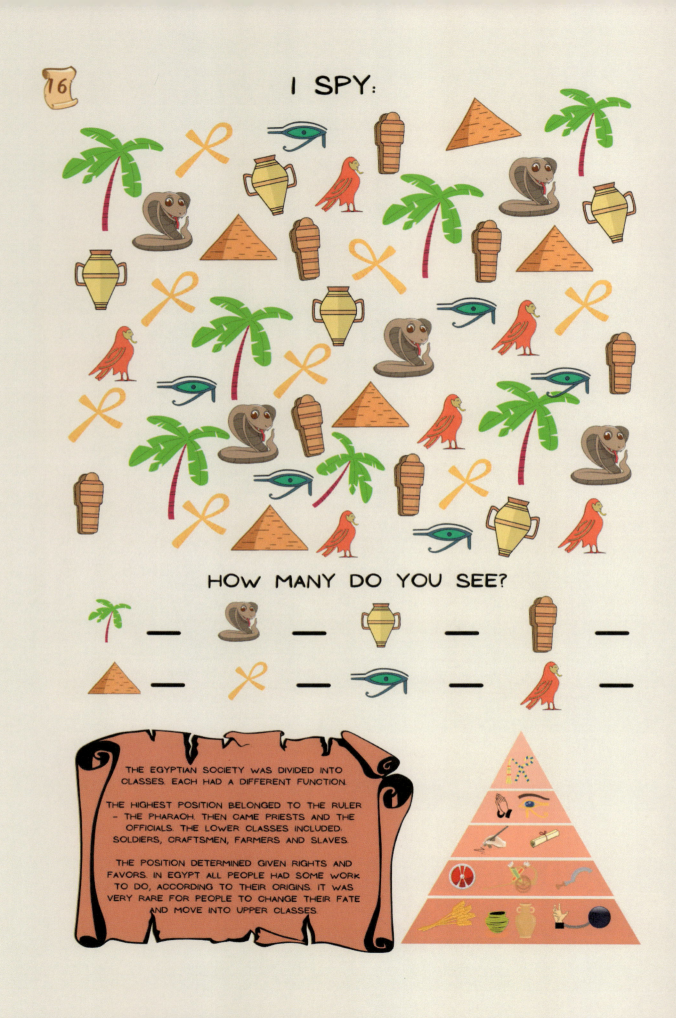

- FOR THE DEAD PHARAOHS PEOPLE BUILT HUGE TOMBS: THE PYRAMIDS.

- BUILDING A PYRAMID TOOK MANY YEARS AND IT REQUIRED THOUSANDS OF WORKERS. THEY USED BIG AND HEAVY BLOCKS OF STONE.

- THE PYRAMIDS WERE DESIGNED IN SUCH A WAY TO PROTECT THE DEAD AND THEIR GOODS FROM THIEVES. ONLY A FEW WORKERS KNEW THE PLAN OF THE PYRAMID. NEVERTHELESS, THE PYRAMIDS WERE OFTEN RIFLED.

- BESIDES THE MUMMY, MANY OTHER ITEMS WERE PLACED IN THERE: FOOD, AMULETS AND OTHER THINGS, NECESSARY IN THE AFTERLIFE.

**17** HELP THE MUMMY ESCAPE FROM THE PYRAMID.

## DID YOU KNOW???

THE GREAT PYRAMID OF GIZA, ALSO KNOWN AS THE PYRAMID OF CHEOPS, IS THE LARGEST OF THEM ALL. THE AMOUNT OF STONE USED TO BUILD IT WOULD BE ENOUGH TO BUILD A WALL AROUND THE STATE OF ARIZONA!

### PYRAMIDS' RECORDS:

| | |
|---|---|
| THE HIGHEST | THE PYRAMID OF CHEOPS (139M) |
| THE OLDEST | THE STEP PYRAMID OF DJOSER 2650 BCE |
| THE BIGEST | THE PYRAMID OF CHEOPS (139M) |

THE EGYPTIAN BUILDERS BUILT NOT ONLY THE PYRAMIDS. MANY TEMPLES, MONUMENTS AND OBELISKS SURVIVED UNTIL THE PRESENT DAYS.

TEMPLE OF HATSHEPSUT DEIR EL-BAHARI

THE TEMPLE OF ABU SIMBEL

18 COLOR THE PICTURE BY NUMBERS.

## DID YOU KNOW ???

IN THE HISTORY OF EGYPT WOMEN COULD ALSO BECAME PHARAOHS. THEY WERE SMART RULERS AND THEY TOOK GREAT CARE OF THE WHOLE COUNTRY.

19 TRACE THE LINES AND WRITE THE CORRECT LETTERS IN THE EMPTY SQUARES.

THE FIRST — HATSHEPSUT
THE LAST — KLEOPATRA VII.
THE MOST BEAUTIFUL — NEFERTITI
THE MOST POWERFUL — NEFERTARI

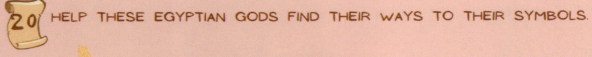 HELP THESE EGYPTIAN GODS FIND THEIR WAYS TO THEIR SYMBOLS.

## DID YOU KNOW???

IN FRONT OF EVERY EGYPTIAN TEMPLE WERE OBELISKS, HIGH AND THIN STONE COLUMNS.

THEY WERE THE SYMBOLS OF THE GLORY OF THE GOD OF SUN. EVEN THE HIGHEST ONES WERE SCULPTED IN ONE PIECE! THE TOP OF THE OBELISK WAS COVERED IN GOLD AND ONE COULD SEE ITS GLOW FROM FAR AWAY.

 CONNECT THE NUMBERS FROM 1 TO 79 AND COLOR THE PICTURE.

FIND TWO IDENTICAL AMULETS AND MATCH THEM TOGETHER.

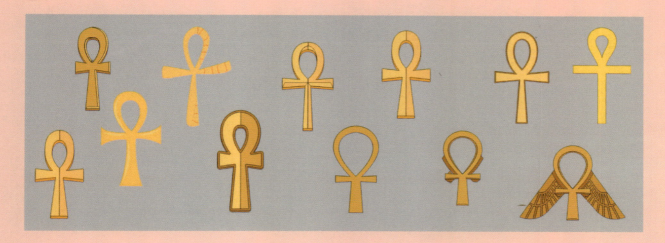

 HELP THESE LITTLE EGYPTIANS GET PAST THE SWAMPS AND REACH THE GROUND.

ABOVE EVERY SNAKE YOU CAN SEE A LETTER. CROSS IT OUT FROM EACH ONE AND WRITE THE REST OF THE LETTERS (STARTING FROM THEIR HEADS) BELOW THE SNAKE. YOU WILL GET THE NAMES OF THE CAPITAL CITIES OF ANCIENT EGYPT.

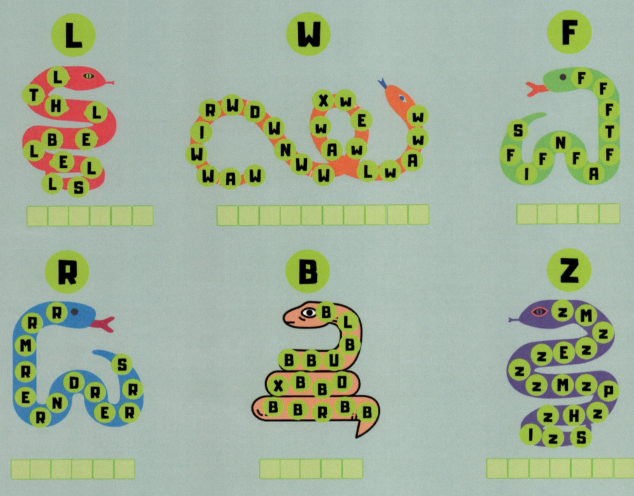

TODAY THE CAPITAL CITY OF EGYPT IS **CARO**

## THE FINAL JUDGEMENT

THE SYMBOL OF MAAT - THE GODDESS OF TRUTH, JUSTICE AND ORDER, WAS AN OSTRICH FEATHER. BEFORE GETTING INTO THE OTHER WORLD, THE DEAD HAD BEEN JUDGED BY OSIRIS, WHO USED THE FEATHER. IF THE HEART OF THAT PERSON WAS LIGHTER THAN THE FEATHER, IT MEANT THAT IT WAS PURE. IF IT WAS HEAVIER, THE DEAD COULDN'T GET INSIDE.

# HOW MUCH DOES IT WEIGH?

USING THE WEIGHTS BELOW, DRAW THE CORRECT ONES ON THE EMPTY SCALES. REMEMBER THAT IF SOMETHING IS HEAVIER ON ONE SIDE THAN FROM THE OTHER SIDE, THE SCALE GOES DOWN.

SOME EXAMPLES HAVE MORE THAN 1 SOLUTION. DRAW ONLY 1. USE THESE WEIGHTS:

ONLY THE PRIESTS COULD STAY IN THE TEMPLES. THEY MADE SACRIFICES, BURNED INCENSE AND READ PRAYERS. THE PRIEST HAD CLEAN, WHITE ROBE, SHAVED HEAD AND HAD TO HAVE A BATH A FEW TIMES A DAY. THAT IS WHY THE EGYPTIANS CALLED THEM "CLEAN".

**26** LOOK AT THE WORD LIST AND CIRCLE THE WORDS IN THE WORD SEARCH.

BANDAGE
ISIS
TEMPLE
RIVER
DYNASTY
CHEOPS
SCARAB
CLEOPATRA
CRAFTSMAN

```
C C R A F T S M A N
C C L E O P A T R A
Y H D Y N A S T Y L
T E M P L E N Y O P
I O L G S R I V E R
S P V A C L T C A R
I S S T A R C C A O
S N Y M R G I R E N
D S R B A N D A G E
M P S E B N F T N R
```

 **27** HELP THE MUMMY GET INTO THE OTHER WORLD.

AN ONION WAS ONE OF THE MOST POPULAR VEGETABLES AMONG THE EGYPTIANS. ITS STRONG SMELL WAS PERCEIVED AS A MAGICAL POWER THAT COULD SCARE AWAY THE BAD GHOSTS. DURING CEREMONIES PEOPLE WORE WREATHS MADE FROM ONIONS.

## DID YOU KNOW???

**TUTANKHAMUN**

HIS TOMB WASN'T DISCOVERED UNTIL THE 20TH CENTURY. IT IS THE ONLY ONE THAT HASN'T BEEN RIFLED. THE ARCHEOLOGISTS FOUND THERE ITEMS SUCH AS: A GOLDEN MASK, A SARCOPHAGUS, MANY PAINTINGS, SCULPTURES, ETC.

THERE IS A LEGEND ABOUT THE "CURSE OF THE PHARAOHS". MANY PEOPLE DIED SHORTLY AFTER WORKING AT THE DIGS. FOR MANY YEARS THE CAUSE OF DEATHS WAS UNCLEAR, BUT NOW THE POSSIBLE REASONS ARE DISEASES CAUSED BY THE BACTERIA INSIDE THE TOMB.

 USE THE EMPTY SQUARES TO WRITE THE LETTERS MATCHING THE PICTURES. THE ANSWER IS THE LOCATION OF TUTANKHAMUN'S TOMB.

**29** THERE IS A PICTURE IN EACH ROW THAT IS NOT THE SAME AS OTHERS. FIND IT!

FILL IN THE BLANKS IN SUCH A WAY THAT EACH ITEM APPEARS ONLY ONCE VERTICALLY AND HORIZONTALLY.

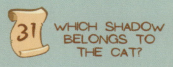 WHICH SHADOW BELONGS TO THE CAT?

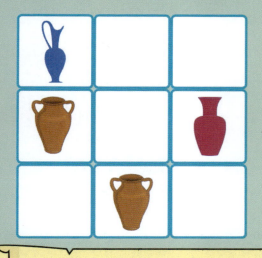

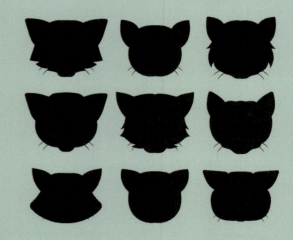

IN ANCIENT EGYPT MANY ANIMALS WERE ADMIRED: CROCODILES, BULLS, SCARABS, IBISES, COWS, BABOONS, FALCONS. CATS WERE SO SPECIAL TO THEM THAT EGYPTIANS EVEN STARTED EMBALMING THEM AND PUT THEM IN BUBASTIS, IN THE TEMPLE OF BASTET, PORTRAYED AS A WOMAN WITH A CAT'S HEAD.

WRITE THE MATCHING WORDS IN THE CROSSWORD. LETTERS IN THE MARKED SQUARES PROVIDE THE ANSWER.

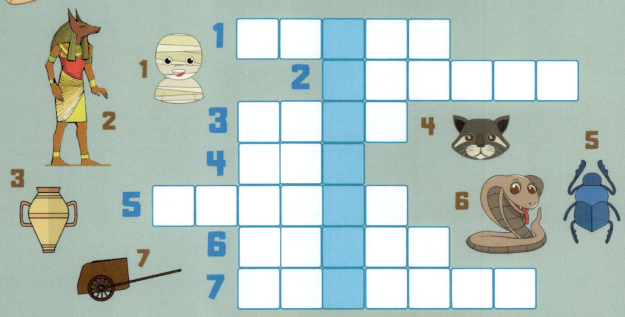

DO YOU KNOW WHAT IT MEANS? CHECK ON THE NEXT PAGE!

DID YOU KNOW???

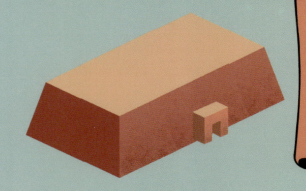

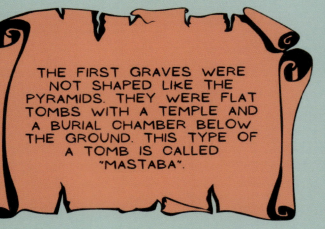

THE FIRST GRAVES WERE NOT SHAPED LIKE THE PYRAMIDS. THEY WERE FLAT TOMBS WITH A TEMPLE AND A BURIAL CHAMBER BELOW THE GROUND. THIS TYPE OF A TOMB IS CALLED "MASTABA".

 LOOK AT THE WORD LIST. CIRCLE THE WORDS IN THE WORD SEARCH.

HATHOR    GODDESS
CAMEL     FUNERAL
SCRIBE    SAHARA
MYTH      KINGDOM
SNAKE

```
S I I G O D D E S S
C A M E L I S S E S
R S A H A R A N O E
I O K I N G D O M O
B T R S N A K E M K
E I E F U N E R A L
N S U N M S A N H N
A F L F Y S I R U H
D H H A T H O R A M
C H G L H R A A S R
```

 USE THE EMPTY SQUARES TO WRITE DOWN THE LETTERS POINTED BY THE ARROWS. WHAT WORD DID YOU GET?

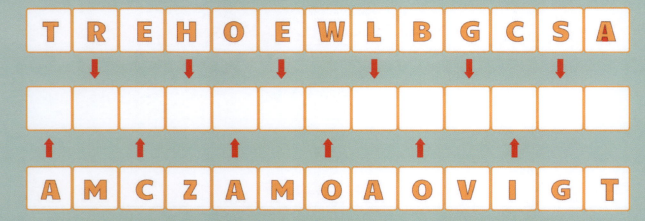

**35** LOOK AT THE WORD LIST. CIRCLE THE WORDS IN THE WORD SEARCH.

PALACE
THOTH
SCALE
IBIS
GRAVE
PLAQUE
MEDICINE
AMULET
BASTET

| M | E | P | I | B | I | S | B | N | A |
|---|---|---|---|---|---|---|---|---|---|
| E | C | E | P | C | T | G | B | A | A |
| D | E | P | L | L | B | R | D | T | T |
| I | H | P | U | Q | L | A | T | V | A |
| C | I | L | A | C | S | V | T | B | A |
| I | P | A | L | A | C | E | H | U | M |
| N | L | Q | S | T | A | S | O | Q | U |
| E | C | U | S | L | L | L | T | S | L |
| C | L | E | T | S | E | H | H | E | E |
| L | B | A | S | T | E | T | U | I | T |

ANCIENT EGYPTIANS CARED ABOUT THEIR APPEARANCE. MEN AND WOMEN WORE WIGS, BRACELETS, EARRINGS AND NECKLACES. THEY USED PERFUME AND EYE SHADOWS. THOSE PROTECTED THEIR EYES FROM THE DESERT WIND. RICH PEOPLE WERE ABLE TO AFFORD EXPENSIVE MIRRORS.

**36** TRACE THE LINES AND HELP THESE WOMEN FIND THEIR HAIR ACCESSORIES.

COLOR THE PICTURE BY NUMBERS.

# I SPY:

# HOW MANY DO YOU SEE?

39 DRAW THE CAMEL STEP BY STEP. THEN TRY TO DRAW IT IN ONE STEP.

AN ADULT CAMEL CAN DRINK MORE THAN 50 GALLONS OF WATER IN THREE MINUTES!

## DID YOU KNOW???

THE AMULETS WERE SMALL ITEMS CARRIED BY THE EGYPTIANS. THEY BELIEVED THAT THEY COULD PROTECT THEM FROM DISEASES, SNAKE BITES OR BRING THEM LUCK.

**SCARAB** — THE SYMBOL OF REVIVAL, OFTEN PUT IN MUMMIES

**ANKH** — THE SYMBOL OF PROSPEROUS, ENDLESS LIFE

**EYE OF HORUS** — THE SYMBOL OF REVIVAL AND RECOVERY

 HELP THE GIRL GET TO HER PRECIOUS AMULET.

41. LOOK AT THE WORD LIST. CIRCLE THE WORDS IN THE WORD SEARCH.

PRIEST
PTAH
SLAVE
PYRAMID
COBRA
RAMSES
HARVEST
SPELL
ROMANS

```
A N S H S O H T S E
H M T P Y R A M I D
A P R I E S T S E R
R A M S E S T P I O
V S L A V E D A B M
E P S R I M T O R A
S E N C O B R A S N
T L V L P E A H S S
S L B O H I P T A H
A V H V M I S A N R
```

IN THE SUNNY EGYPT ONE IS ALWAYS FOLLOWED BY THEIR SHADOW. EGYPTIANS BELIEVED THAT IT IS A SYMBOL OF A SOUL, WHICH LIVES TOGETHER WITH THE SUN AND AFTER DEATH, IT WILL TURN INTO A BIRD.

42. WHICH SHADOW BELONGS TO THE PHARAOH?

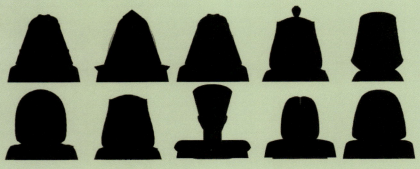

43. MATCH THE IDENTICAL MUMMIES. IF A MUMMY HAS NO PAIR, DRAW A CIRCLE AROUND IT.

COUNT THE ITEMS AND FILL IN THE BLANKS WITH CORRECT NUMBERS.

44

ANCIENT EGYPTIANS WERE VERY GOOD AT MATHS. THEY DIDN'T HAVE CALCULATORS AND THEY HAD TO DO THE COUNTING BY THEMSELVES. LET'S PRACTICE WITH THEM!

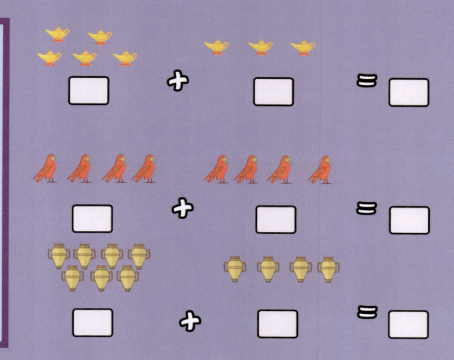

 45 CONNECT THE DOTS FROM 1 TO 50 AND THERE YOU WILL SEE A PICTURE OF AN EGYPTIAN GOD

MEDICINE IN EGYPT WAS VERY WELL DEVELOPED. THE DOCTORS TREATED MANY ILLNESSES AND THERE WERE MANY SPECIALISTS: OPHTHALMOLOGISTS, DENTISTS ETC., BUT THEY ALSO GREW MEDICINAL PLANTS AND PRODUCED MEDS. THEY USED ABOUT ONE-THIRD OF THE MEDS WE KNOW TODAY.

BESIDES ODD SPECIFICS SUCH AS HIPPO FAT,  CHILD'S URINE, THEY USED MEDICINES  PRODUCED FROM PLANTS, FOR EXAMPLE GARLIC OR  ONION. TO PROTECT THEMSELVES FROM GETTING  A DISEASE PEOPLE USED AMULETS AND BURNED INCENSE.

**46** HELP THE CROCODILE GET TO THE NILE.

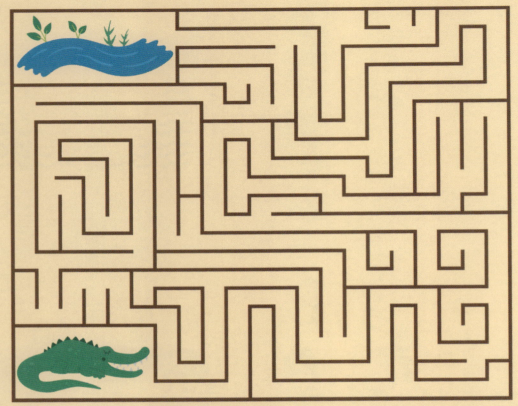

IN EGYPT YOU CAN MEET A DUNG BEETLE. THEY LIVE UNDER THE GROUND BUT LEAVE THEIR HOUSES TO ROLL BALLS OF MANURE. THAT IS WHY PEOPLE BELIEVED THAT IT IS A SYMBOL OF RISING SUN, WHICH IS VERY SIMILAR TO SUCH A BALL, AS IF SOMEONE WAS HITCHING IT THROUGH THE SKY.

**47** LOOK AT THE WORD LIST. CIRCLE THE WORDS IN THE WORD SEARCH.

HORUS
MAAT
CROWN
SPHINX
MUMMY
DONKEY
PAPYRUS
ANKH
WRITING

```
W N W W H M Y H I D
R I H O R U S U M P
I M A A T M M D P A
T U P Y Y M N O R P
I I O C S Y P N H Y
N D N P P A N K H R
G G Y A H T O E O U
N Y R N I N I Y T S
C R O W N H A O U P
A P R Y X I W N N A
```

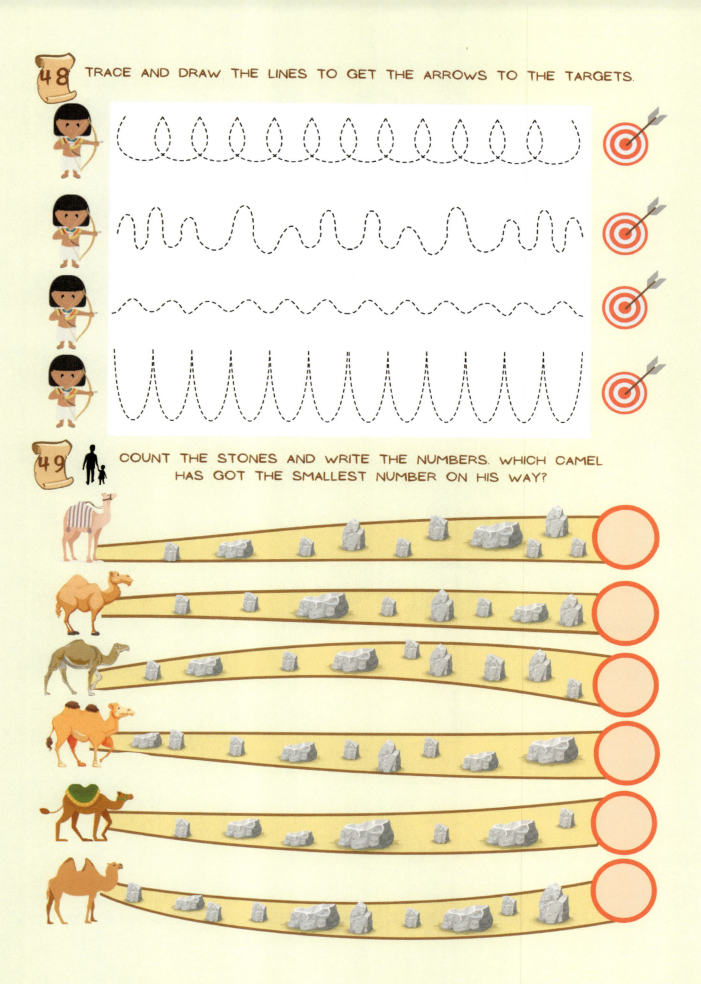

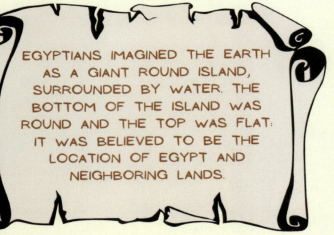

EGYPTIANS IMAGINED THE EARTH AS A GIANT ROUND ISLAND, SURROUNDED BY WATER. THE BOTTOM OF THE ISLAND WAS ROUND AND THE TOP WAS FLAT: IT WAS BELIEVED TO BE THE LOCATION OF EGYPT AND NEIGHBORING LANDS.

 FIND 8 DIFFERENCES BETWEEN THESE PICTURES.

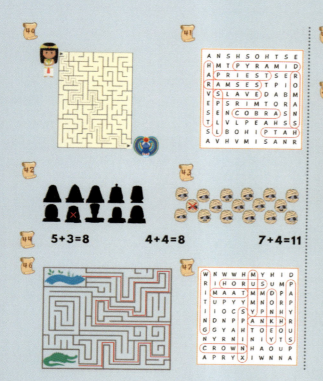

5+3=8    4+4=8    7+4=11

Printed in Great Britain
by Amazon